SILLY JOKES FOR 10 YEAR OLDS

Why was the space man so happy?

He was feeling over the moon.

What do llamas say after they finish a yoga session?

Llamaste.

What did the music teacher use his ladder for?

To help him reach the high notes.

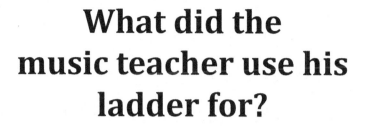

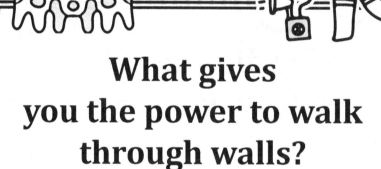

What gives you the power to walk through walls?

Doors.

How can you make sure you get straight A's?

Use a ruler.

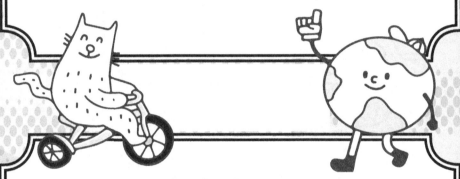

Why did the prince need to visit the dentist?

Because he broke his crown.

Wow! You've grown really tall. You'd better not grow another foot!
Why ever not?
Because if you did, your mom will need to buy you a third shoe!

A butcher wears a size 12 shoe and a size XXL shirt, so what does he weigh?

Meat.

What do you create when you throw a load of books in the ocean?

A title wave.

What do snowmen wear to get around?

Ice skates.

What did the shore say to the tide that finally came in?

Long time, no sea.

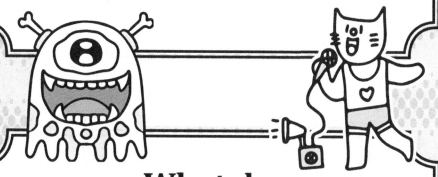

What do royals drizzle over their pancakes?

Sir Up.
(syrup)

What do grandpas do if you tell them they need to change their hearing aid?

They don't listen.

How can you stop a raging bull from charging?

Unplug it.

What does Santa Claus experience when he gets stuck going down a chimney?

Santa Claustrophobia.

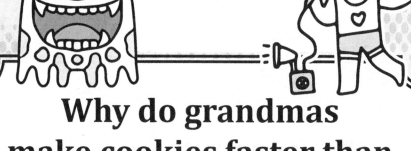

Why do grandmas make cookies faster than anyone?

Because they only take nana-seconds to bake them.

What should you do when your teacher rolls her eyes at you?

Scoop them up and roll them back.

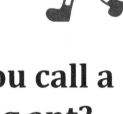

What would you call a crime-fighting ant?

A vigil-ant-e.

Why don't ants get sick?

They have too many anti-bodies.

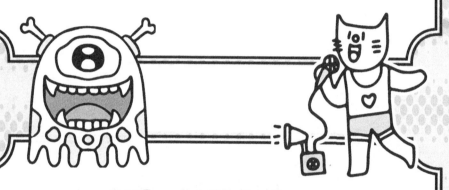

What did the frustrated sharpener tell the pencil?

Stop going round in circles and get to the point!

Which llama is the greatest of all spiritual leaders?

The Dalai Llama, of course.

What do you call it when someone eats their alarm clock?

A time-consuming activity.

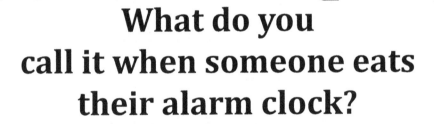

What would you call a fly without wings?

A walk!

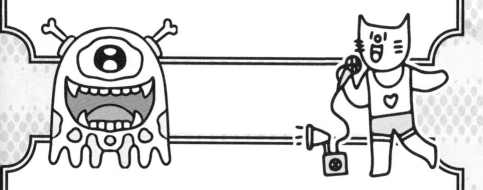

Why couldn't the koala bear get a job?

He kept being told he was over-koala-fied.

Mom, all the teachers at school keep saying I'm easily distracted.

Well I think you might be Timmy; you live in the house across the street.

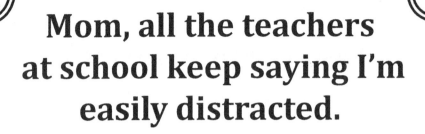

What made the man run around his bed?

He needed to catch up on sleep.

What would a broken plate say when buying a cupcake?

I need this to be glue-ten free please.

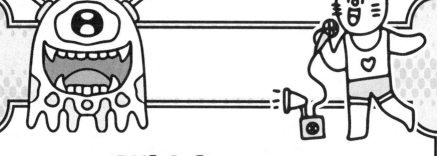

Which store does Cupid buy his arrows from?

Target.

Why don't cows have feet?

Well, they lac-toes, you see.

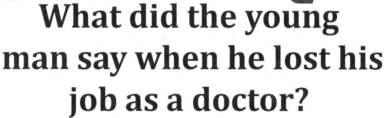

What did the young man say when he lost his job as a doctor?

"I never had enough patience."

Where do mosquitoes go during winter?

I don't know, but I would love if they stayed there in summer too.

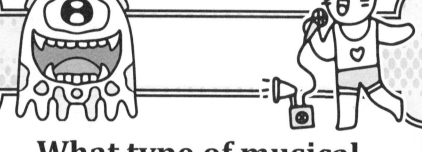

What type of musical instruments do cats play very well?

Purrrr-cussion instruments.

When does the rain sometimes give you money?

When there is a change in the weather.

How do most fleas travel around the country?

By itch-hiking.

Why shouldn't you tell a cow anything important?

It just goes in one ear and out the udder.

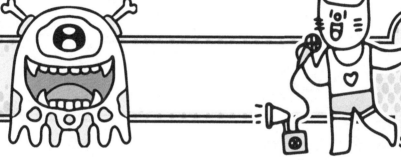

Why did the teacher tie all of the children's shoe laces together?

So they could have a class trip.

What type of kitten works in a hospital?

A first-aid kit.

Which letter do pirates love?

You'd think it was R, but their first love is the C!

Why did the farmer's son choose not to study medicine?

Because he wanted to enter a different field.

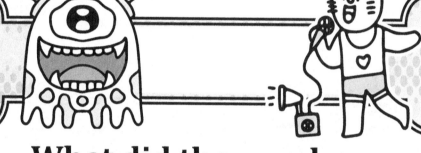

What did the envelope tell the stamp before they got posted?

Just stick with me and we'll go places!

What never asks questions but always gets answered anyway?

A cellphone.

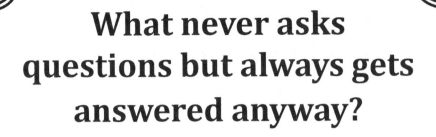

Why did the clever girl refuse to spell 'part' backwards?

She knew it was a trap.

How can you tell when your cat has used your computer?

Your mouse will have teeth marks on it.

Which bird was the most famous in boxing history?

Muhammad Owli.

Why did the man get fired from the calendar factory?

He was taking too many days off.

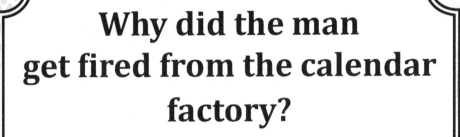

Knock, knock.
Who's there?
Theodore.
Theodore who?
Theodore was ajar so I let myself in.

Which aunt is the penguins' favorite?

Aunt-Arctica.

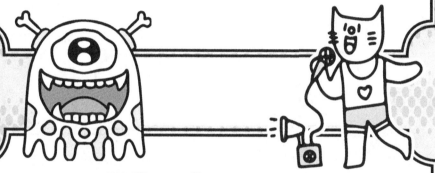

Why do most Swedish ships come with barcodes?

So that ports never forget to Scanda-navy-in.

Why do owls usually go to church?

Because they are bird of prey.

What begins with E, ends with E and only has a single letter in it?

Envelope.

What did people say when Nikola Tesla and Isaac Newton said the same thing at the same time?

Great-est minds think alike.

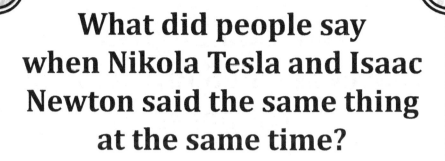

Knock, knock.
Who's there?
Honeydew.
Honeydew who?
Honeydew know where I left my keys?

What do English teachers call Santa's Little Helpers?

Subordinate clauses.

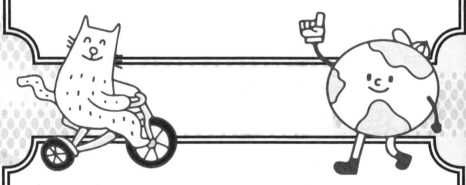

What did the teacher say to the boy who threw a lump of cheddar in class?

That's not very mature.

Will we see February March?

No, but I think April May.

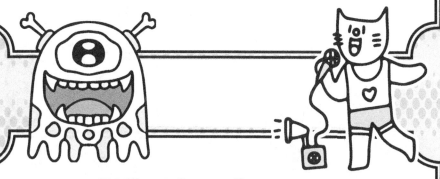

Why is a horse different to wet weather?

One rains down and the other is reined up.

What would you call a guy lying down on your doorstep?

Matt.

Why did the sun not need to go to college?

It already has a million degrees.

Why did the cat not need to visit the vet?

She was feline pretty fine.

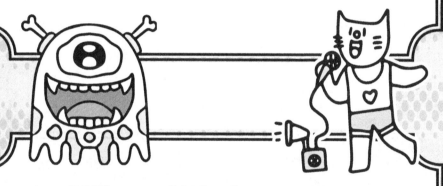

What did the critic say about the new moon restaurant?

The food is great, but there's no atmosphere.

Why did the quarterback choose very difficult classes?

He always knew he would pass.

Why did the skeleton walk into the restaurant?

To get some spare ribs.

What made the man store his money in the freezer?

He needed some cold hard cash.

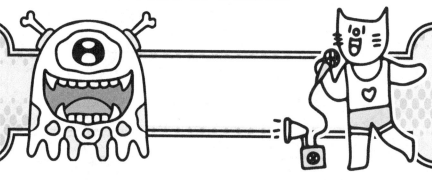

What did the big brother flower say to the little brother flower?

Hey, bud.

What would you call a polar bear that stole calamari?

A squid-napper.

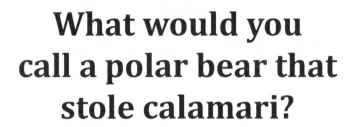

How do you tell if a rabbit is very old?

Look for grey hares.

Where is the warmest place to go in a room when you're cold?

The corners - they're usually 90 degrees.

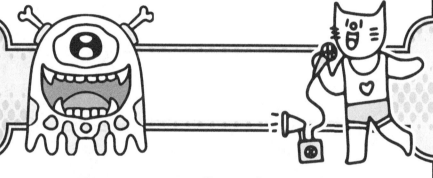

Do you think this pool is safe to dive into?

Hmm. That deep ends.

Why are cats so good at getting what they want?

They have great powers of purrr-suasion.

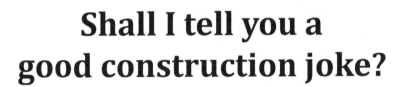

Shall I tell you a good construction joke?

Sorry I can't, I'm still working on it.

What did one mindreader say to the other?

"You are fine, how am I?"

What did the man say when his friend got crushed under a pile of books?

"I'm afraid he's only got him-shelf to blame"

What did the buffalo mom say to her son when she dropped him at school?

Bison.

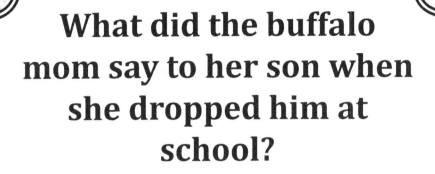

What made the baby ant feel so confused?

All of his uncles were ants.

What is the most popular sport among elves?

North-pole vaulting.

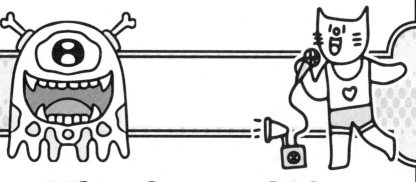

What do most kids give their parents for Christmas?

A list of the things they want.

What gets harder to catch when you run faster?

Your breath!

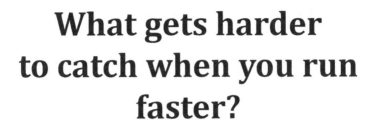

Knock, knock.
Who's there?
Hike.
Hike who?
Ooh, I didn't know you liked Japanese poetry.

Why can't a nose be twelve inches long?

Because then it would be a foot.

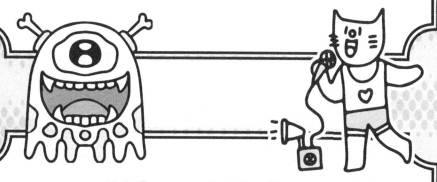

What did the football coach scream at the broken vending machine?

"Give me my quarter back!"

What is always in front of you, but can't be seen?

The future.

How would you lift an elephant with one hand?

Don't worry; you'll never find an elephant with one hand.

How do you tell if someone is a great farmer?

They are out-standing in their field.

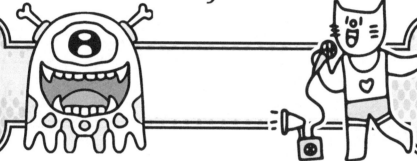

What would you get if you crossed a sheepdog with a tulip?

A collie-flower.

Which shoes are the strongest kind?

Under Armor shoes.

How does the barber give the moon a haircut?

Eclipse it.

What should you do if an astronaut gets upset?

Give them some space.

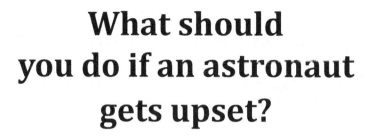

Which type of fruit do vampires love the most?

Blood oranges.

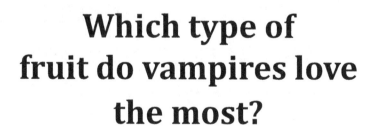

What did the judge say during the skunk's trial?

"Odor in the court, odor in the court!"

How can you sneak a mythical creature into your apartment?

Through the Gryffindor!

What do computers usually eat for lunch?

Anything that they can byte.

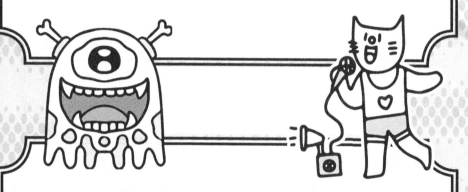

What did the bird ask his co-worker?

"What's your opinion of the stork market lately?"

Why did the origami teacher leave her job?

She got fed up with the paperwork.

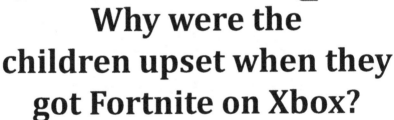

Why were the children upset when they got Fortnite on Xbox?

It only lasted two weeks.

What made the neighbor's cat so small?

It only drank condensed milk.

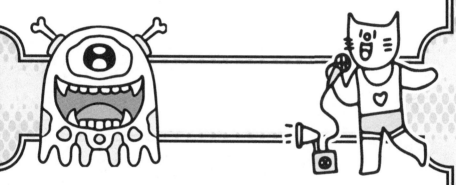

What did the chef say to the man who asked if they were serving noodles?

"Yes, of course, sir, we serve everyone here."

Which is the only area of math that owls love?

Owl-gebra.

Why couldn't the elephant get a job?

All of his qualifications were irrelephant.

What do snowmen and snowwomen call their kids?

Their chill-dren.

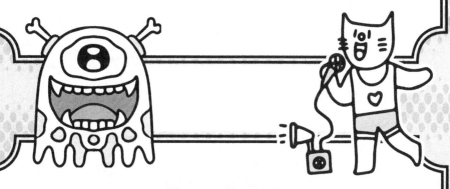

Why don't basketball players get to go on vacation?

They would always get called for traveling.

Why could cyclops never be a teacher?

He'll never have more than one pupil.

Why did people think the echo was being rude?

Because it kept answering back.

Which three letter word starts with gas?

Car.

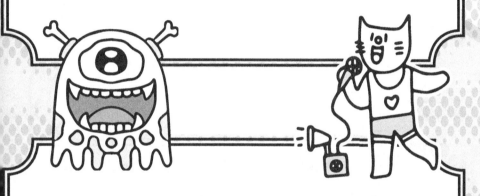

Which place in New York do math teachers love to visit?

Times Square.

What occurs just once in a lifetime, twice in every moment, but never in one hundred years?

The letter 'M'.

Why do cornfields have such amazing hearing?

Because they have so many ears.

Why did the politician get out of breath?

She was running for office.

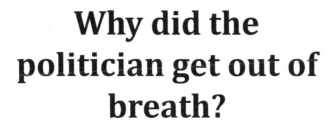

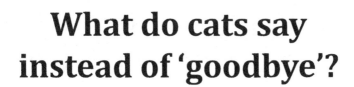

What do cats say instead of 'goodbye'?

"See ya litter."

What would you get if you mixed a Christmas tree with an iPhone?

A pine-Apple.

Why shouldn't you interrupt someone who's concentrating on a word puzzle?

They'll probably have some cross words for you.

What did Steve Jobs always order at McDonald's?

A Big Mac.

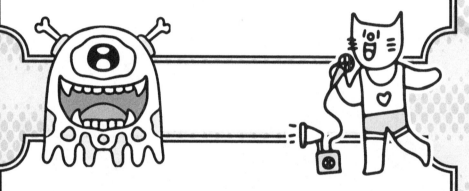

What did the geologist say to her team?

"Stop taking my work for granite."

How can a boy go for 25 days without sleep?

He can just sleep at night.

Why do witches love staying in fancy hotels?

They enjoy the excellent broom service.

Why is a crazy rabbit different to a fake dollar bill?

One is a mad bunny, the other is bad money.

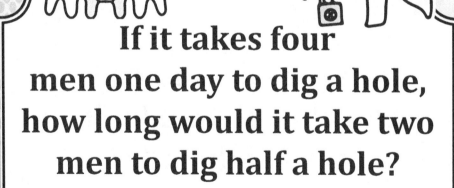

If it takes four men one day to dig a hole, how long would it take two men to dig half a hole?

There's no such thing as half a hole.

Where do they make average and okay products?

At the satisfactory.

What could you call a rabbit that always looks on the bright side?

A hop-timist.

Why is Valentine's Day very popular among skunks?

They are rather scent-imental creatures.

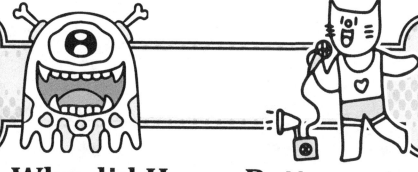

Why did Harry Potter get confused between his best friend and his potion-mixing pot?

They are both cauld Ron.

Why was Will Smith one of the coolest photographers?

He made Fresh Prints.

What is even worse than raining cats and dogs?

Hailing taxis!

Where can you find a dog that has no legs?

Wherever you left her

When is a roast duck very bad for your health?

When you are the duck.

Guess what my French friend said when I asked if she played video games.

"Wii."

Why are dogs similar to telephones?

They both have collar IDs.

What do they call a sleepwalking nun?

A roamin' Catholic.

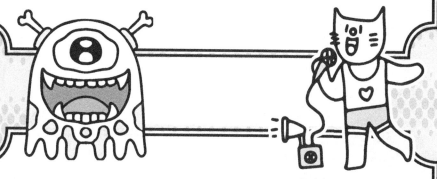

Why are scrambled eggs similar to a losing baseball team?

They both got beaten.

Why did the scientist fear telling a chemistry joke?

She thought she might not get a reaction.

Why did the tiny ghost get recruited to the football team?

They needed a little team spirit.

Why wouldn't Cleopatra visit a psychiatrist?

She was Queen of Denial.

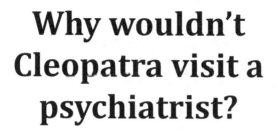

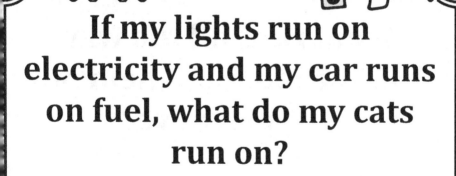

If my lights run on electricity and my car runs on fuel, what do my cats run on?

Their paws.

Which historical Chinese cat was the most powerful?

Chairman Meow.

What runs all the way around a football field but doesn't move?

A fence.

What do they call babies that join the army?

The infantry.

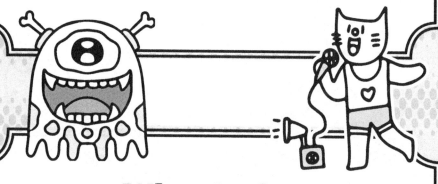

What is the Capital of Spain?

The letter 'S'.

What did the cat say when the dog ate all of its food?

"You've just gotta be kitten me..."

Why do robots never feel afraid?

Because they have nerves of steel.

What did Leonardo, Donatello, Raphael and Michelangelo say about Master Splinter?

"He tortoise so much."

Why are skeletons awful at Fortnite?

They don't have any skins.

What do you call two boys that love doing algebra together?

Algebros.

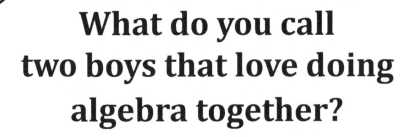

Where can you usually find ghosts on a football field?

Under the ghoul posts.

Why didn't the skeleton want to play football?

His heart just wasn't in it

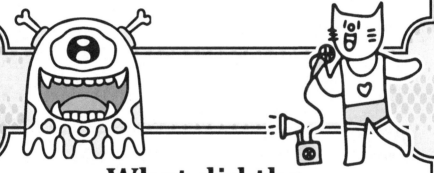

What did the long-tailed macaque say when its tail got stuck in a blender?

"It won't be long now..."

Where do most spiders put their silk up for sale?

On their website.

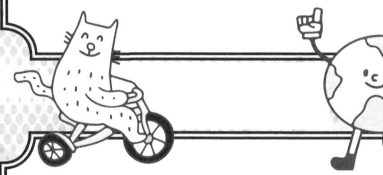

Why do all shoemakers get to heaven?

They have such good soles.

Which state do football players visit when they need new uniforms?

New Jersey.

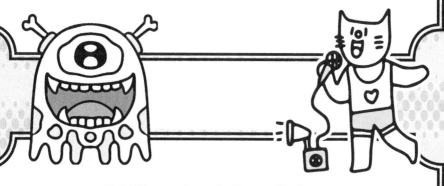

Why is 'dark' spelled with a 'k' not a 'c'?

Because you can't c in dark!

Made in United States
North Haven, CT
05 February 2025

65418312R00046